WITHDRAWN
BY
WILLIAMSBURG REGIONAL LIBRARY

MAY -- 2014

PAPERING
WALLS & CEILINGS

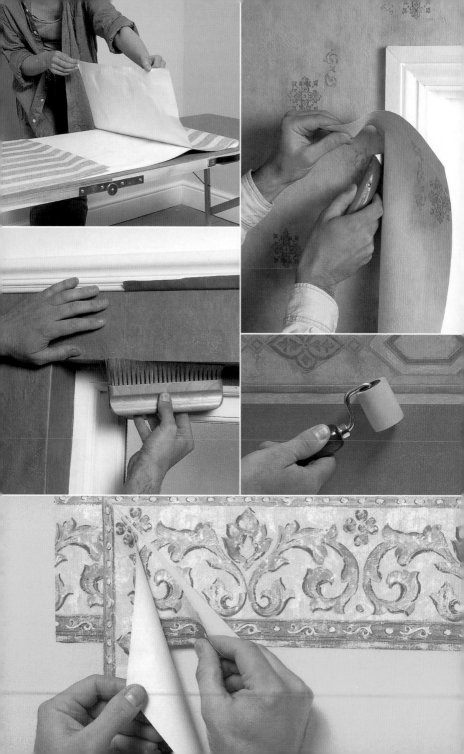

PAPERING

WALLS & CEILINGS

Diane Carr

Contributing Editor: Ian Penberthy

LORENZ BOOKS

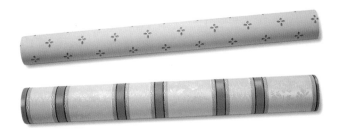

This edition is published by Lorenz Books,
an imprint of Anness Publishing Ltd,
Blaby Road, Wigston,
Leicestershire LE18 4SE;

info@anness.com

www.lorenzbooks.com;
www.annesspublishing.com

If you like the images in this book and
would like to investigate using them for
publishing, promotions or advertising,
please visit our website
www.practicalpictures.com for more
information.

© Anness Publishing Limited 2013

Publisher: Joanna Lorenz
Editors: Felicity Forster, Anne Hildyard
Photographer: Colin Bowling
Illustrator: Peter Bull
Designer: Bill Mason
Production Controller: Mai-Ling Collyer

NOTES
The author and publishers have made every
effort to ensure that all instructions
contained within this book are accurate and
safe, and cannot accept liability for any
resulting injury, damage or loss to persons
or property, however it may arise. If in any
doubt as to the correct procedure to follow
for any home improvements task, seek
professional advice.

CONTENTS

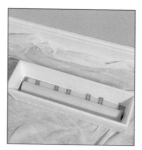

INTRODUCTION

Fifty years ago, practically all of the rooms of almost every home would have had papered walls, and many would have had papered ceilings too. When decorating, few people would have even considered not hanging wallpaper; it was how things were done. In more recent times, however, the popularity of wallcoverings has diminished, and today many look upon them as a more luxurious finish to be reserved for the more important rooms in the home. That said, modern wallcoverings – not all of which are paper based – are far more versatile than their forerunners, offering not only a wide range of colours and patterns, but also in some cases high wear and moisture resistance, making them particularly suitable for kitchens, bathrooms and children's rooms, where traditional wallpapers would not be an ideal choice.

Many of today's do-it-yourselfers may be put off by the thought of hanging a wallcovering. But hanging wallcoverings is actually quite a straightforward task that, in the main, requires only care to achieve very professional-looking results.

While it is true that wallcoverings are not as popular as they once were, there is no doubt that a well-chosen example

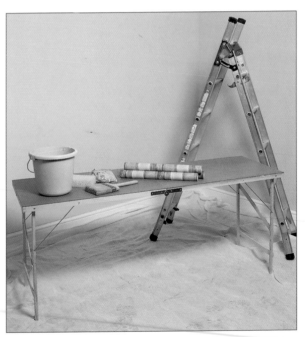

LEFT: Hanging wallcoverings requires the use of a few specialized tools, which are readily available. You will also need an inexpensive folding pasting table and at least one set of sturdy stepladders.

ABOVE: When joining border papers that have intricate patterns, professional results can be achieved by cutting around a prominent shape in the pattern and butting the ends together.

While practically all wallcoverings are printed by machine, handprinted examples are still available, often offering traditional patterns. Not surprisingly, they are expensive, but for the restoration of a period property they offer the perfect decorative solution.

You don't need many special tools for hanging wallcoverings, unlike many other do-it-yourself jobs: pasting and hanging brushes, some paperhanger's scissors and a pasting table, all of which are inexpensive. With this equipment, a roll of wallpaper and this book, you'll soon be giving your rooms a new look.

can give a far more impressive finish to a room than paint alone. Whether you want a subdued delicate pattern, a wildly flamboyant design, muted colours or bold tones, there will be a wallcovering to meet your needs. Moreover, you need not restrict yourself to flat coverings either, since there is a good choice of textured materials to be had. As with colours and patterns, textures may be light or heavy, and several can be over-painted, offering even greater decorative possibilities.

There are special finishes, too, that may be based on foils, fabrics and natural materials such as grasses. While these are more difficult to hang than conventional wallcoverings, they may be just what is required to add a final feature to a decorative scheme.

AVOIDING PASTE DRIPS

A length of string tied tightly across the top of a wallpaper paste bucket makes a handy brush rest. Use the string rather than the side of the bucket for removing excess adhesive from the pasting brush.

MATERIALS &
EQUIPMENT

These days, there are wallcoverings for every room in your home, offering a wide choice of colourways, patterns and textures. Some offer good wear resistance, and many are washable. So when considering this type of decorative finish, the first decision to make is what type of wallcovering suits your needs; then you can select from the colours and patterns on offer. Estimating quantities is important, as you don't want to end up with too many rolls; equally, too few could cause problems, as subsequent rolls you buy may come from later batches and display colour differences. Fortunately, estimating is a simple task. You will need some special tools and equipment, but these are widely available.

CHOOSING WALLCOVERINGS

Wallcoverings offer a wide range of patterns and colourways, from very traditional to the most modern designs. Choose with care, particularly if you are new to hanging wallpaper, as some will be much easier to hang than others. Check the manufacturer's guidelines before buying to determine the suitability of the paper.

BUYING WALLCOVERINGS

When shopping for wallcoverings, ask for a large sample of any design that catches your eye so you can examine it in the room that is to be decorated. Look at the samples in both natural and artificial light, near a window and in a dark corner, as some colours and patterns alter dramatically when viewed in different lights.

Test a sample for durability by moistening it under a tap. If it tears easily or the colours run when rubbed lightly, the paper could be difficult to hang and maintain. Avoid thin papers, particularly if you are an inexperienced decorator, as they are likely to tear when moistened by the paste and may be difficult to hang.

Never skimp on the number of rolls you buy, and check that the batch number on all rolls is the same, as there may be a slight colour variation between batches that may not be noticeable on the roll, but could become obvious after hanging. However, the batch system is not infallible, so check rolls again for a good colour match before cutting and hanging. It is also worth buying at least one extra roll. Many retailers offer a sale-or-return service.

CHOOSING A PATTERN

Take a critical look at the room you plan to decorate and make a note of any aspects that could make hanging a wallcovering difficult. Uneven walls and

ABOVE: A freematch wallpaper or one with a continuous pattern, such as stripes, will not need an allowance for pattern matching.

ABOVE: A straight-match pattern has the same part of the pattern running down each side of the paper, making the cutting of drops simple.

ABOVE: An offset pattern has motifs staggered between drops, which must be taken into account when cutting and measuring the paper.

awkward corners, for example, can make pattern matching particularly problematic, while some types of wallcovering will conceal a poor surface better than others.

Regular patterns, such as vertical stripes, checks and repetitive geometric designs, will emphasize walls that are out of true, whereas random florals and paint-effect papers will not encourage the eye to rest on any one point and, therefore, will help to disguise awkward angles. Trimming can also ruin the appearance of a large pattern, so in a room that has a sloping or uneven ceiling, or several windows, cabinets and doors, a design with a small pattern may be a better choice. If a poor surface is the problem, avoid thin or shiny wallcoverings, which will highlight every blemish.

If you are not an experienced decorator, avoid complicated patterns, as any mismatching will be obvious; instead consider using one of the many easy-to-hang, freematch designs that are readily available.

BELOW: Wallcoverings are available in many different designs and finishes, so choose with care.

ESTIMATING QUANTITIES

Standard wallcoverings are sold in rolls that measure approximately 10m long by 530mm wide (33ft x 21in). Use the tables to calculate the number of rolls that you require for walls and ceilings, remembering to add 10 per cent for waste, especially if the design has a large pattern repeat. Lining paper is usually 560mm (22in) wide and is available in standard 10m (33ft) and larger roll sizes. You can calculate the number of rolls required from the tables, but there is no need to add any extra for a pattern repeat. For walls, measure around the room and include all the windows and doors in your calculation, except for very large picture windows and patio doors. It is easier to measure the perimeter of the floor to calculate the size of a ceiling.

Depending on where they were manufactured, you may find papers in non-standard sizes, so do check. This could well be the case with hand-made wallcoverings. These often have the added complication of an unprinted border down each edge, which must be removed before hanging, although some suppliers may be able to do this for you. In the USA, wallcoverings vary in width and length, but are usually available in rolls sized to cover specific areas.

In fact, it is not that difficult to calculate your requirements for a non-standard wallcovering. When papering walls, measure the height of the wall first and divide the length of a single roll by that figure. This will give you the number of drops you can cut from a single roll. Multiply that number by the width of the roll to determine the width of wall that will be covered by a roll. Then divide the total width of all the walls to be covered by that figure. This will give you the total number of rolls needed. As before, include windows and doors and add 10 per cent for waste.

If in any doubt, approach your supplier; many will be happy to make the calculation for you.

CALCULATING THE NUMBER OF ROLLS NEEDED FOR A CEILING

MEASUREMENT AROUND ROOM		NUMBER OF ROLLS
10m	(33ft)	2
11m	(36ft)	2
12m	(39ft)	2
13m	(43ft)	3
14m	(46ft)	3
15m	(49ft)	4
16m	(52ft)	4
17m	(56ft)	4
18m	(59ft)	5
19m	(62ft)	5
20m	(66ft)	5
21m	(69ft)	6
22m	(72ft)	7
23m	(75ft)	7
24m	(79ft)	8
25m	(82ft)	8

LEFT: Measuring up for wallcovering. Measure the height of the walls and their total width. Then refer to the tables to determine the number of standard-size rolls required. There is no need to deduct the area of doors and windows, unless they are very large. If you want to paper the ceiling, it will be easier to measure the floor to calculate the area.

CALCULATING THE NUMBER OF ROLLS NEEDED FOR WALLS

HEIGHT OF ROOM FROM SKIRTING (BASEBOARD)

WIDTH OF WALLS	2–2.25m (6ft 7in–7ft 5in)	2.25–2.5m (7ft 5in–8ft 2in)	2.5–2.75m (8ft 2in–9ft)	2.75–3m (9ft–9ft 10in)	3–3.25m (9ft 10in–10ft 8in)	3.25–3.5m (10ft 8in–11ft 6in)	3.5–3.75m (11ft 6in–12ft 4in)	3.75–4m (12ft 4in–13ft 1in)
	NUMBER OF ROLLS							
10m (33ft)	5	5	6	6	7	7	8	8
11m (36ft)	5	6	7	7	8	8	9	9
12m (39ft)	6	6	7	8	8	9	9	10
13m (43ft)	6	7	8	8	9	10	10	10
14m (46ft)	7	7	8	9	10	10	11	11
15m (49ft)	7	8	9	9	10	11	12	12
16m (52ft)	8	8	9	10	11	11	12	13
17m (56ft)	8	9	10	10	11	12	13	14
18m (59ft)	9	9	10	11	12	13	14	15
19m (62ft)	9	10	11	12	13	14	15	16
20m (66ft)	9	10	11	12	13	14	15	16
21m (69ft)	10	11	12	13	14	15	16	17
22m (72ft)	10	11	13	14	15	16	17	18
23m (75ft)	11	12	13	14	15	17	18	19
24m (79ft)	11	12	14	15	16	17	18	20
25m (82ft)	12	13	14	15	17	18	19	20

BASIC WALLCOVERINGS

When choosing a wallcovering, it is important to take into consideration how practical it will be in the room you wish to decorate. Each room in your home has different requirements and by choosing the right type of wallcovering, you will be sure of a decorative surface that will wear well and look good for many years.

LINING PAPER

This provides a smooth base for wallpaper or paint on walls and ceilings. It is made in several grades from light 480 grade, suitable for new or near-perfect walls, to extra-thick 1200 grade for use on rough and pitted plaster. A good-quality lining paper will be easier to handle than a cheap, thin paper and less likely to tear when it has been moistened by paste.

WALLPAPERS FOR PAINTING

Woodchip paper is made by sandwiching particles of wood between two layers of paper. The thicker grades are easy to hang and cover uneven surfaces quite well, but woodchip paper is not easy to cut and can be hard to remove, while thinner grades tear easily. Woodchip paper is a budget buy, but it is not attractive or durable.

Relief wallpaper is imprinted with a raised, decorative surface pattern and comes in many designs, as well as pre-cut dado (chair rail) panels and borders. It is easy to hang, although thinner grades can tear when wet. It hides blemishes and is durable once painted.

Textured vinyl has a deeply embossed surface pattern that masks flaws and is uncrushable, so it is suitable for hardwearing areas such as the hall (lobby) and children's rooms. It is more expensive than relief wallpaper, but is very easy to hang and usually dry strippable.

Embossed wallcovering comes in rolls and pre-cut panels made from a solid film of linseed oil and fillers fused on to a backing paper. It requires a special adhesive and will crack if folded. It is very expensive, but is extremely hardwearing and durable, and the deeply profiled, traditional designs are particularly suited to use in older and period properties. It can also be painted over.

IMPORTANT CONSIDERATIONS

While woodchip and relief papers are ideal for disguising minor blemishes and irregularities in the wall surface, they cannot be used to hide an uneven or poor-quality surface. This should be borne in mind when choosing the wallcovering, and steps should be taken to make good any substantial damage, or an unstable surface, before hanging.

In addition, the heavier types of embossed wallcovering require special hanging techniques that may, in the long run, make it preferable to repair the wall and use a more conventional wallcovering. For example, some types may require the wall to be covered with lining paper first, and

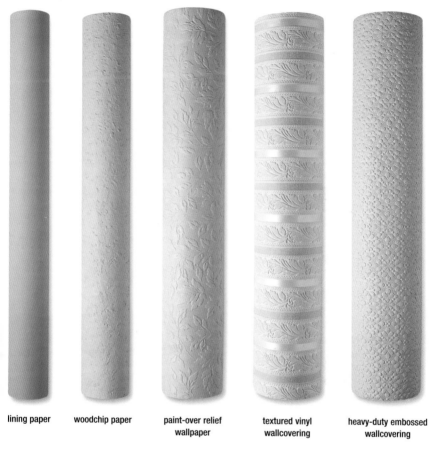

| lining paper | woodchip paper | paint-over relief wallpaper | textured vinyl wallcovering | heavy-duty embossed wallcovering |

soaking times can be quite long. The back of some papers must be thoroughly soaked with hot water before applying paste. These papers are very stiff and must be handled with care; they cannot be folded, as this would break the relief pattern, leaving a permanent mark.

A seam roller cannot be used, as this would flatten the edges between drops, damaging the relief pattern and making the joins between drops really obvious. Instead, careful work with a paperhanger's brush is required to ensure that edges are pressed down. Because the papers cannot be folded, they cannot be brushed around internal and external corners. Therefore, drops must be cut to fit exactly up to the angles; at an external corner, the join must be disguised by applying a small amount of conventional cellulose filler (Spackle) once the paper has dried.

PRINTED WALLCOVERINGS

Printed wallcoverings offer a wide variety of designs and finishes to suit every situation in your home. Choose them with care.

PATTERNED WALLCOVERINGS

Printed wallpaper is available in an extensive choice of patterns and colours. The cheapest are machine-printed, but top-price designs are hand-printed and often untrimmed, so hanging is best left to the professionals. Printed wallpaper can be sponged, but is not particularly durable and is best used in rooms where it will not be subjected to much wear. The thinner grades tear easily when pasted.

Washable wallpaper also comes in a good choice of designs, but is more durable and has a thin plastic coating that allows the surface to be washed clean when necessary. It is priced competitively, is fairly easy to hang and in some cases is dry strippable.

Vinyl wallcovering has a very durable surface layer of PVC that creates a hardwearing, often scrubbable, finish that resists steam, moisture and mould. There is a good choice of colours and patterns, as well as pearlized and embossed textured designs. Vinyl wallcovering is usually ready-pasted and dry strippable; paste-the-wall ranges are also available.

Sculptured vinyl is a thick, very hardwearing vinyl imprinted with a decorative design or tile effect. The waterproof finish resists steam, condensation, grease and cooking splashes, so it is a good choice for kitchens and bathrooms. It requires a heavy-duty adhesive, but is easy to hang and is dry strippable.

When buying wallcoverings, check the labels carefully to determine whether the covering you like will be suitable for the situation in which you want to hang it. If in doubt, seek the advice of your supplier. He or she will also be able to tell you if any special adhesives or hanging techniques will be required for what you have in mind. Be wary of opting for "fashionable" patterns, particularly if they are flamboyant, as they may soon lose their appeal.

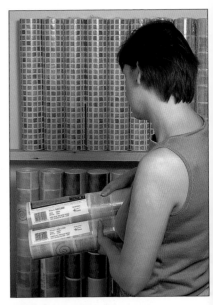

ABOVE: Some wallcoverings are more hardwearing than others. Bear this in mind when choosing a pattern and material.

| printed wallpaper | vinyl wallcovering | paste-the-wall wallcovering | sculptured vinyl wallcovering |

SPECIAL WALLCOVERINGS

Metallic foils and wallcoverings made from natural materials such as cork, silk and grasscloth can often be ordered from dedicated decorating outlets. They are expensive and difficult to hang, so employing a professional is advisable. In general, they are hard to clean, so they are best for low-wear areas of the home.

Some special wallcoverings will actually hide minor imperfections in the wall surface; others will highlight them, so choose with care.

special metallic wallcoverings

WALLCOVERING EQUIPMENT

Using the correct tools will make the job of hanging wallcoverings much easier, allowing you to achieve a more professional finish. Some are needed specifically for wallcovering; others are likely to be part of your standard do-it-yourself tool kit. When buying decorating tools of any type, always opt for quality rather than quantity – to make sure they last longer and produce better results.

MEASURING AND MARKING

A retractable steel tape is essential for taking accurate measurements, while a long metal straightedge, a spirit (carpenter's) level and a pencil will be needed for marking levels, vertical guidelines on walls and the positions of fixtures.

CUTTING AND TRIMMING

For cutting wallcovering to length and trimming edges, you will need a pair of paperhanger's scissors, which have long blades and curved tips used for creasing paper into angles. Choose scissors that are at least 250mm (10in) long and made from stainless steel, or have been specially coated so that they will not rust.

A sharp craft knife can also be used for trimming and will be easier to use with vinyl wallcoverings. Various trimming tools are available too, including the roller cutter, which enables you to crease and cut into edges with a single movement, and is accurate and simple to use.

PASTING

For mixing and applying paste, you will need a plastic bucket and a paste brush. Paste brushes have synthetic bristles and will be easier to clean than paintbrushes. A pasting table is not essential, but is useful. It is cheap and fold for easy storage. For ready-pasted wallcoverings, a polystyrene (Styrofoam) soaking trough is required.

HANGING

To ensure that wallcoverings are hung straight and true, a plumbline and spirit (carpenter's) level are essential tools. Hanging wallcoverings may also involve working at heights, so access equipment will be required. A set of sturdy steps will be suitable for papering walls, but a safe work platform or movable workstation will be needed for tackling ceilings and stairwells.

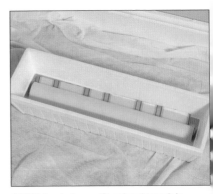

ABOVE: A polystyrene (Styrofoam) trough is needed for soaking ready-pasted wallcoverings. This will allow you to carry each drop to where it will be hung, and help to keep water off the floor.

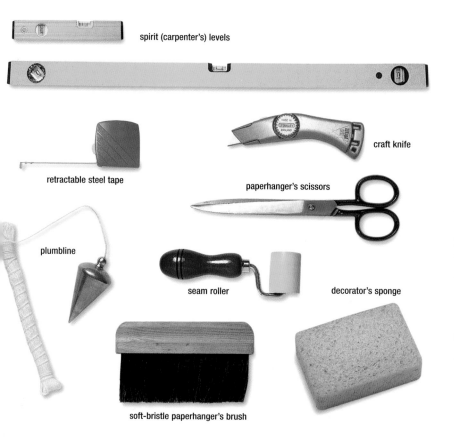

spirit (carpenter's) levels

craft knife

retractable steel tape

paperhanger's scissors

plumbline

seam roller

decorator's sponge

soft-bristle paperhanger's brush

FINISHING

A paperhanger's brush is the best tool for smoothing down wallpaper, although a sponge can be used for vinyl wallcoverings. For the best results, choose a brush with soft, flexible bristles and buy the largest size that you can manage comfortably. Do not use wallpaper brushes with a metal ferrule or collar on them for this job, as you might inadvertently tear or mark delicate wallcoverings.

Use a cellulose decorator's sponge rather than an ordinary household sponge. This type of sponge is made of a higher-density material, which is firmer and will hold water better. It can also be used for washing down walls before papering or painting.

A seam roller will give a neat finish to joints and the edges of borders, making sure they are stuck down well, but should not be used on wallpaper with an embossed pattern. Various types made from wood and plastic are available. A soft plastic seam roller is best, as it is less likely to leave marks on thin or over-pasted wallpapers.

ACCESS EQUIPMENT AND SAFETY

Most wallcovering jobs involve the use of a stepladder, which should be tall enough to allow you to touch the ceiling easily. For papering ceilings you need to set up a proper platform across the width of the room at a comfortable height. Do not step from chair to chair or set up similar makeshift arrangements.

AVOIDING ACCIDENTS

Steps and ladders can be hazardous, so make sure they are in good condition. Accessories to make a ladder safer to use include the ladder stay, which spreads the weight of the ladder across a vertical surface to prevent slippage; and the standing platform, which

provides a more comfortable and safer surface to stand on. Even more stable is the movable workstation or a board or staging slung between two pairs of steps or trestles. These can often be used with a safety rail.

CONSTRUCTING A WORK PLATFORM FOR STAIRS

To construct a stair platform, you will need a strong stepladder, a straight ladder and a sturdy scaffold board that is long enough to reach between the two. If you need to bridge a gap of 1.5m (5ft) or more, two scaffold boards placed one on top of the other will be needed, and if the span is greater than 2.4m (8ft), the centre of the boards will require additional support.

The planks should be tied securely to each ladder with stout rope. If the platform has to be erected over balustrading, make sure that the feet of the straight ladder are wedged firmly in place: a strip of wood screwed to one of the stairs is the safest method.

WORK PLATFORMS

A work platform can be made from trestles and sturdy boards. For comfort, adjust the platform so that the top of your head is around 300mm (12in) from the ceiling.

TIPS

• Protect the staircase walls from damage by padding the ends of the straight ladder with soft cloths held with tape.
• Where a banister rail is screwed to the wall, try to plan the lengths so that the fixing falls at a butt joint.
• A strip of wood screwed to one of the stairs will ensure that the feet of a ladder do not slip.

make sure the foot of
the ladder is secure

LEFT: How to construct a work platform for a staircase with a landing.

ABOVE: A movable workstation simplifies the whole process.

SAFETY TIPS

• Never over-reach when working on steps or a ladder; climb down and reposition it.

• Never allow children or pets into areas where power tools or strong solvents are being used.

• Do not work when you are overtired. This causes lapses in concentration, which can lead to silly, expensive and/or dangerous mistakes.

• Keep the work environment tidy. Flexes (power cords) should not be walked on or coiled up tightly, because it damages them internally. Moreover, trailing flexes can be a trip hazard and long extension leads (cords) can be prone to overheating.

• Wear protective clothing, including a dust mask and goggles, when preparing walls for papering.

PREPARATION

As with any decorative scheme, wallcoverings rely on the quality of the surface to which they are applied for their final appearance. While some papers and vinyls are thick and will disguise minor irregularities in a wall or ceiling, most will not, so it is essential to repair all surface defects if you want the finish to look its best. Although an existing sound papered finish can be papered over, it is far better to remove the old covering and apply the new one to a clean surface. And if that surface is dusty, it should be washed off and sealed so that the wallpaper paste can adhere well. For some wallcoverings a lining paper should be hung on the wall first to provide the best finish.

REMOVING TEXTURED FINISHES

If the wall or ceiling to be given a new covering is painted or wallpapered, preparing the surface for its new finish is quite straightforward. However, if it was previously covered with materials such as texture paint, ceramic or polystyrene (Styrofoam) tiles or wall panelling, more work will be needed to remove the old finishes and return the surface to its original condition.

Textured finishes are tackled in different ways, depending on their type. Texture paints are basically thick water-based paints, normally used to create relatively low-relief effects, and can be removed with specially formulated paint removers. Some textured effects formed with a powder or ready-mixed compound are best removed with a steam wallpaper stripper, which softens the compound so that it can be scraped from the wall.

Never attempt to sand off a textured finish. There are two reasons. The first is that it will create huge quantities of very fine dust; the second is that older versions of this product contained asbestos fibres as a filler, and any action that might release these into the atmosphere as inhalable dust must be avoided at all costs.

PRACTICAL CONSIDERATIONS

Whichever method you use for stripping old texture paint, it will be messy, so you must take steps to protect yourself and areas of the room that you are not working on. Preferably wear overalls; at the very least old clothes. Rubber gloves are a must, as is some form of eye protection if you are working on a ceiling, while the latter is also essential when using a chemical stripper. A hat will keep your hair clean.

Ideally, remove all furniture from the room, but if you can't or don't want to do this, place it all together in the centre of the room and cover it with dust sheets (drop cloths). When working on a ceiling, you will have to move the furniture to another part of the room at some stage. Cover the floor with dust sheets, too, and provide yourself with a supply of plastic bags for collecting the paint scrapings. Bear in mind that chemical strippers can give off toxic fumes, so open windows to ensure good ventilation, but close doors to other rooms to prevent the fumes from spreading through your home. Make sure you clean up before leaving the room to prevent tracking paint scrapings through the house.

Always follow the instructions given with a chemical stripper, allowing the required soaking time before scraping off the softened paint. In some areas, you may need a second application of stripper to remove all the paint. Don't cover too large an area at one time, as this will cause an unnecessary build-up of fumes. You should be able to get into a rhythm of scraping one area while the stripper soaks into the next. Make sure you wash off all traces of stripper before hanging your paper.

REMOVING TEXTURED FINISHES

1 Strip off old texture paint by brushing on a generous coat of a proprietary texture paint remover using an old paintbrush. Stipple it well into the paint and leave it to penetrate for the specified amount of time.

2 When the paint has softened, scrape it off with a broad-bladed scraper. At all times, wear gloves and also safety goggles as protection against splashes.

3 Once the bulk of the coating is removed, use wire (steel) wool dipped in the paint stripper to remove any remaining flecks of paint.

4 Remove powder-based or ready-mixed types using a steam stripper, which will soften the finish. Never try to sand off this type of finish.

REMOVING TILES AND PANELLING

For tiles and wall panelling, complete removal or a cover-up with plasterboard (gypsum board) are the two options available. The former will leave a surface in need of considerable renovation, while the latter will cause a slight loss of space within the room, as well as some complications at door and window openings. If you are faced with removing a layer of ceramic tiles from a wall, it is unlikely that you will be able to do so without causing a fair amount of damage to the surface below. In this situation, it will be better to add a skim coat of fresh plaster to the entire surface, rather than try to make good individual areas of damage. Unless you are confident that you can achieve a perfectly flat finish, entrust this work to a professional plasterer.

REMOVING WALL PANELLING

1 The last board to be attached will have been nailed to the fixing grounds through its face. Use a hammer and nail punch to drive the nails right through the board and free it. Lift it off the wall.

REMOVING CERAMIC TILES

1 On a completely tiled wall, use a hammer to crack a tile and create a starting point for the stripping. On partly tiled walls, start at the tile edge.

2 Use a broad bolster (stonecutter's) chisel and a club (spalling) hammer to chip the old tiles off the wall.

2 The other boards will have been secret-nailed through their tongues. Use a crowbar (wrecking bar) to prise them away from their grounds, taking care not to cause too much damage to the wall.

3 Finally, prise the grounds off the wall. Use a claw hammer with some protective packing to lever them out of the wall. Some nails may come away with the grounds; others may be left in the wall.

REMOVING POLYSTYRENE (STYROFOAM) TILES

1 Lever the tiles away from the ceiling with a scraper. If the tiles were fixed with a continuous coat of adhesive, consider fitting a new ceiling.

2 If the tiles were stuck in place with blobs of adhesive, use a heat gun to soften the old adhesive so it can be removed with a scraper.

REMOVING OLD WALLPAPER

Although a sound wallcovering can be papered over, it is far better to remove all traces of it.

REMOVING WALLPAPER

Ordinary wallpaper is not difficult to remove and requires only wetting and soaking for 10–15 minutes before stripping with a broad-bladed scraper. Adding wallpaper stripper or a few drops of washing-up liquid (dishwashing detergent) to the water will help it to penetrate the paper. Wallpaper that has been over-painted or has a washable finish needs scoring with the edge of a scraper before soaking, but hiring a steam stripper is the easiest method, and you are less likely to damage the plaster surface.

If walls are faced with plasterboard (gypsum board), take care not to saturate the surface or hold a steam stripper in place for too long. Dry-strippable papers can simply be peeled from the wall, leaving the backing paper in place. If this is still adhering well and remains intact, a new wallcovering can be hung over the top, but if it tears, the backing should also be removed.

PREPARING SURFACES

Once all the old paper has been removed, walls should be washed thoroughly with a solution of sugar soap (all-purpose cleaner) to remove dust, grime and traces of old adhesive.

Rinse and allow the surface to dry. Cracks and gaps should also be repaired, and any stains that remain after cleaning should be sealed. For settlement cracks between walls and the ceiling or woodwork, use a flexible decorators' filler, and seal stains with an aluminium primer or proprietary aerosol stain block.

New porous plaster and old walls that are dusty will require sealing. A PVA adhesive (white glue) solution of one part PVA to five parts water is ideal for sealing these surfaces and will stabilize them before papering. A coat of size or heavy-duty wallpaper paste ensures good adhesion of the wallcovering and allows paper to be manoeuvred freely on the wall.

PREPARING WALLS

1 Use abrasive paper wrapped around a sanding block to remove any remaining "nibs" of wallpaper.

ABOVE: Stubborn wallpaper will be easier to remove with a steam stripper. You can hire one if you don't expect to be doing much stripping.

ABOVE: Vinyl wallcoverings can usually be stripped dry and will peel off the wall, leaving the backing behind; strip this off if it tears.

2 Repair any cracks with cellulose filler (Spackle) and seal persistent stains with a stain block or aluminium paint.

3 A coat of size will make the wallpaper easier to hang on new plaster; it prevents moisture being absorbed too quickly from the paste.

HANGING LINING PAPER

Lining paper helps to disguise surface blemishes and provides a good surface for decorating. It is usually hung horizontally so that the joints do not coincide with those of the decorative paper, but hanging vertical lengths will be easier in narrow alcoves and where there are wall fixtures such as pipes. On poor walls, two layers of lining paper may be necessary; the first layer should be hung vertically, and the second horizontally.

The basic paperhanging techniques shown on the following pages can also be used for lining paper, but it should be left to soak for only five minutes to become pliable. Treat each surface separately and trim the paper to fit into internal and external corners. Do not use a ceiling as a guideline, expecting it to be level; mark a horizontal guideline for the lower edge of the first length (immediately below the ceiling) with a spirit (carpenter's) level and long straightedge. If you are lining both walls and ceiling, start with the ceiling, working from one end of the room to the other.

Work from right to left if right-handed and left to right if left-handed, folding each length of lining paper concertina-fashion to make it manageable. Allow a slight overlap on to the adjacent wall at each end and on to the ceiling if this is uneven. When the paper has been

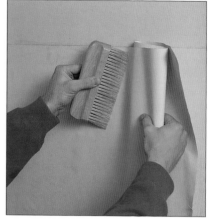

1 Normally, lining paper is hung in horizontal lengths across each wall, preventing the joints from coinciding with those of the decorative paper, as this could cause them to open up as the paste dries.

brushed out, crease these overlaps with the back of the scissors, peel back and trim to the crease before brushing back. Work down the wall, trimming the last length so that it butts against the top edge of the skirting (baseboard).

TIPS

• Allow at least 24 hours for lining paper to dry out completely before hanging the final wallcovering.
• Lining paper may shrink as it dries. Fill small gaps between lengths with fine surface filler and sand smooth. In corners, use a bead of flexible filler (Spackle) and smooth with a wet finger.

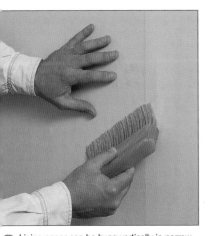

2 Lining paper can be hung vertically in narrow alcoves or behind pipework, however, if this makes the job easier. It should also be hung vertically if you intend over-painting it, as the joins will be less obvious.

3 To line a ceiling, work across the longest dimension of the room, marking an initial guideline. You may find it easier if someone else holds the concertina of pasted paper while you brush it into place.

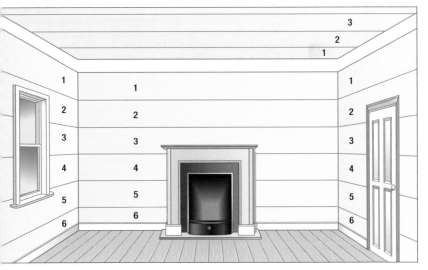

ABOVE: The correct sequence of work when hanging lining paper: for a wall, begin just below the ceiling and move downward; for a ceiling, work across the longest dimension from one end of the room to the other. In each case, trim the last length to width.

WALLPAPERING TECHNIQUES

Contrary to what many people think,
hanging wallpaper is actually quite a
simple process. You do need to take care,
though, since you will be dealing with
long strips of wallcovering, which in
practically all cases will be covered in sticky
paste on one side. The potential for mishaps
is quite high, so work in an unhurried,
logical manner, keeping the work area tidy.
The following pages show you all the
techniques you need to know to paper
walls and ceilings successfully, and how
to cope with difficult areas, such as
corners, doors, windows and alcoves.
Common problems are described,
together with the methods for
overcoming them.

PREPARING WALLPAPER

Wallpaper can be hung using one of three methods, depending on whether you are using a ready-pasted, paste-the-wall or traditional unpasted paper. However, the most important step with any paperhanging task is to prepare fully before cutting the paper by carefully measuring the lengths and making an allowance for pattern matching to avoid mistakes.

PREPARING UNPASTED PAPER

Measure the height of the wall from the ceiling to the top of the skirting (baseboard) and add 100mm (4in) for trimming the top and bottom. Measure and cut the first drop to length. To ensure a square cut, lay the paper flush with the long edge of the pasting table and use a straightedge to mark the cutting line.

If the ceiling is quite level, you can cut a number of lengths. Match the pattern of each length dry off the roll against the first cut length to avoid problems with pattern matching as the job progresses.

Use the paperhanger's brush to weigh one end down, and line up the edge of the paper with the edge of the pasting table, then apply a thin, even coat of paste brushing outward toward the edges.

Fold the ends of the pasted length in to the centre and leave it to soak, checking the manufacturer's guidelines for the exact length of time. Long lengths of paper should be lightly folded concertina-style.

READY-PASTED PAPER

To activate ready-pasted papers, fill a trough two-thirds with water and put it on the floor at the end of the pasting table. Roll a length of paper with the decorative face inside and immerse for the recommended soaking time. Draw it on to the pasting table, patterned side down so that excess water can drain into the trough.

For paste-the-wall papers, apply a coat of paste to an area wider than the paper – it can be hung directly from the roll or using cut lengths.

PREPARING PRE-COATED WALLCOVERINGS

You can buy many wallcoverings pre-coated with adhesive. The adhesive is activated by soaking a length of paper in a trough of cold water. Once immersed and soaked for the recommended length of time, drain the paper into the trough. Mix ordinary paste to recoat any dry edges.

CUTTING, PASTING AND FOLDING WALLPAPER

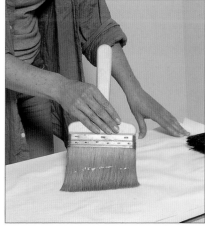

1 Measure carefully, allowing for pattern matching, and cut the paper to length. Cut several more drops from the same roll and to the same length, marking their tops.

2 Brush on an even coat of paste, working out from the centre to the edges. Align each edge with the table edge in turn to prevent paste from getting on to the table.

3 When you have pasted about half of a short drop, fold the pasted end into the middle. Then slide the paper along the table and paste the rest. Fold the end in to meet the first.

4 Fold longer lengths of wallpaper concertina-fashion to make them more manageable. Leave the folded drops of paper for the required time so that the paste soaks in.

HANGING THE FIRST LENGTH

In a room with no focal point, work clockwise around the room. Start and finish near the least obtrusive corner so that any pattern mismatch will not be obvious.

To ensure the end result is well balanced, centre a pattern over a chimney breast (fireplace projection) or other prominent feature and work outward in both directions.

WHERE TO START

Use a plumbline and spirit (carpenter's) level to mark a guideline on the wall. The distance from a corner to the guideline should be one roll width less 25mm (1in), and the first length should be hung so that you are working away from (and not into) the corner.

HANGING THE PAPER

Place the first length next to the guideline, then adjust the top so that there is 50mm (2in) of paper lapping on to the ceiling and slide the vertical edge into its final position.

Lightly brush out the top half of the paper, working downward to expel air bubbles and firmly push the top trimming allowance into the angle with the ceiling. Make sure that the vertical edge is aligned with the guideline then continue to work down the wall, brushing outward from the centre of the length.

Crease the paper into the junction between wall and ceiling by running the blunt edge of the scissors along the

paper, then gently peel back the paper and trim neatly to fit along the creaseline. Brush the trimmed edge firmly back into position.

Ease the bottom half of the paper away from the wall and smooth it into place. Make sure that it is aligned with the guideline, then crease the bottom edge of the paper into the skirting (baseboard) and trim to fit, as before, using scissors.

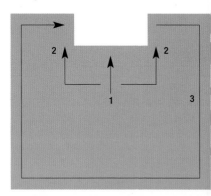

ABOVE: Begin by centring a pattern over a prominent feature, then work outward in both directions.

TIPS

• Hang papers with a large design so that any loss of pattern occurs at floor level, not at the ceiling.
• Agitate pre-pasted papers during soaking to expel any air bubbles and ensure that all the paper comes into contact with water. Make sure the paper is loosely rolled.
• Edges can dry out during trimming – keep a little extra paste handy.

1 Place the edge of the first drop against the vertical guideline, making sure that it is aligned accurately. When you are happy, begin brushing the paper on to the wall.

2 Brush out the top half of the length and push it into the angle with the ceiling, using a dabbing action with the paperhanger's brush. Make sure you brush out all air bubbles.

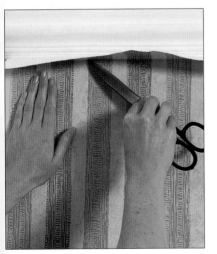

3 Using the back edge of the scissors blade, run along the wall/ceiling angle to crease the paper into it. This will provide an accurate trimming line.

4 Gently peel back the paper and cut along the crease line to remove excess paper. Then brush the end of the drop back into place. Repeat at the skirting (baseboard).

EXTERNAL CORNERS

Corners are unlikely to be completely square, so never try to hang a full width of wallpaper around them as it will not hang straight. Hanging two separate lengths of paper and overlapping them slightly at the corners will produce a far better result, although some small loss of pattern will be inevitable on walls that are not perfectly true.

PAPERING AN EXTERNAL CORNER

Hang the cut length as usual, matching the pattern down the full length, then lightly brush the paper around the corner. Do not apply too much pressure, as the paper could tear, but make sure that there are no bubbles and the paper has adhered well along the edge of the corner.

Use scissors to make a release cut top and bottom where the wall meets the skirting (baseboard) and ceiling. This will allow the paper to be smoothed on to the wall on both sides of the corner and trimmed along the skirting and ceiling. Using a craft knife, trim the length vertically to leave an overlap of about 25mm (1in) brushed around the corner. Discard the waste.

Cut another length and hang this to a vertical guideline on the second wall so that it overlaps the strip of paper brushed around the corner, with its edge about 12mm (½in) from the corner and the pattern matching as closely as possible.

To do this, you may need to hang the new length so that it overlaps the previous length substantially. The width of the pattern will determine how much the two lengths may have to be overlapped. Make a vertical cut with a craft knife through both layers, from ceiling to skirting. Pull away the waste strip of the overlapping drop, then carefully peel back the edge of that drop until you can remove the waste strip of the overlapped drop. If necessary, add a little more paste, then brush back the paper to leave a neat butt join between the two drops. Finally, trim to fit the top and bottom as normal.

When working with a very thin paper, especially if it has a white ground, you can simply leave one drop overlapping the other at an external corner. This will not be very noticeable. However, if you are hanging a vinyl wallcovering, you must make the vertical cut through both drops to produce a butt join, as the pasted overlapping drop will not adhere to the vinyl surface of the drop below, unless you use special overlap adhesive.

If the wall is not completely square, the pattern may not match exactly along the full drop where the two lengths cross over. This cannot be avoided and should be taken into account when planning the order of the work. Always aim for the overlap to be where it is least noticeable. On a chimney breast (fireplace projection), for example, the overlaps should be on the side walls, not the face.

1 Hang the last drop on the first wall and brush the wallpaper smoothly around the external corner.

2 Make vertical release cuts at the top and bottom, into the skirting (baseboard) and ceiling junctions.

3 Trim off the excess paper to leave an overlap of about 25mm (1in). Make sure the edge is brushed down firmly.

4 Hang the first drop on the second wall so that it overlaps the turned paper and the pattern matches as closely as possible.

5 When working with a thick paper or a vinyl wallcovering, make a single cut down through both layers using a sharp knife. Keep the cut as straight as possible.

6 Peel back the edges, remove the waste and brush the edges back into place. You should be left with a neat butt join and minimal disruption to the pattern.

INTERNAL CORNERS

As with external corners, internal corners should be papered with two separate pieces of wallpaper, overlapping them slightly.

Hang the last full-width length, then measure the distance from the edge of the paper into the corner, taking measurements from the top, centre and bottom of the wall. Add a 12mm (½in) overlap allowance to the widest measurement and cut a strip of this width from the next full length. Do not discard the offcut (scrap) – put it to one side for use later.

Hang the cut length, brushing the overlap allowance on to the adjacent wall. Make sure the paper is brushed firmly into the corner by dabbing the wallpaper into the angle with the tips of the brush bristles.

Measure the width of the offcut and use a plumbline to mark a vertical guideline on the adjacent wall that distance from the corner.

If the internal corner is badly out of true, take measurements from the top, centre and bottom of the wall, and adjust the guideline for the offcut so that it will not overlap on to the previous wall.

Hang the offcut against the guideline, overlapping the strip of paper turned on to the wall. Although there will be a slight mismatch of the pattern, it should not be too noticeable. Trim the top and bottom of the length neatly with scissors. Treat a vinyl in the same manner as for an external corner, or use overlap adhesive.

1 When you come to an internal corner, hang the last full-width drop, then measure from the edge of the wallcovering into the corner at the top, middle and bottom.

TIPS

• If an overlap allowance puckers in an internal corner, make small horizontal cuts in the paper so that it lays flat.

• Keep a tube of overlap adhesive handy to ensure that overlapping edges of vinyl wallcoverings adhere properly.

• Paper with a straight-match pattern can be difficult to align in an internal corner. Hold a spirit (carpenter's) level horizontally across the corner to check that the design is level.

2 Using the widest of the three measurements, and adding an allowance to turn around the corner, cut a strip from the next pasted length of paper. Do not discard the waste length.

3 Hang the strip of paper, butting its edge up to the last drop hung and brushing the overlap allowance on to the facing wall. Make sure to brush it well into the corner.

4 Measure the width of the waste length cut from the drop and make a mark at this distance out from the corner. Use a plumbline to position a vertical guideline at this point.

5 Hang the offcut against the line, overlapping the strip turned around the corner and making sure that the edge is brushed down well. Trim at top and bottom.

AROUND DOORS

If you follow the correct sequence for hanging and trimming the lengths of wallpaper, you should be able to paper around a door frame with little trouble.

Mark out the walls in roll widths first so that you know exactly where each length falls. Thin strips beside a door or window will be difficult to hang and are likely to peel, so adjust the starting point if necessary, perhaps moving it half a roll's width in one direction or the other. When you are happy that you will not be left with awkward strips on either side of the door, begin hanging full drops in the normal manner. Continue until you have hung the last full drop before the door.

Hang a full length so that it overlaps the architrave (trim), matching the pattern to the last length hung. Lightly brush the paper on to the wall where possible, and then use the bristle tips of the brush to press the paper into the top of the architrave. Take great care not to tear the wallcovering at this point, particularly if you are using a thin paper.

Locate the external corner of the door frame and make a diagonal release cut into this point with scissors. As you cut toward the corner, press the paper against the wall to prevent it from tearing. Smooth the paper down the wall and brush the vertical overlap of paper into the edge of the architrave. Brush out the section of paper above the door frame, pressing it into the wall/ceiling angle and the angle between architrave and wall.

Make sure the paper does not separate from the previous length as you do this. Crease the paper against the architrave with the back of the scissors, then ease the paper away from the wall and cut along the creases, or trim with a craft knife held at a 45-degree angle to the wall. Trim the top of the door frame first, cutting inward from the outer edge of the architrave. Brush the paper back into place against the side and top of the architrave. Then crease the paper against the ceiling and trim it to fit. Wipe the paste from the woodwork and the paper. Hang the next drop in a similar manner, butting it against the last drop above the door and making a release cut so that it will fit around the frame. Trim and brush into place.

TIPS

• Lightly smooth the pasted paper on to the wall before trimming so that it does not tear under its own weight when it is damp.
• The junction between wall and door frame is rarely even; trimming the paper so that it overlaps the frame slightly will create a much neater finish.
• If the sides of a reveal are uneven, trim overlapping paper to 50mm (2in) and make horizontal release cuts down the length so that it lies flat, then cut a separate strip to fit.
• Complete all cutting and trimming around doors and windows first, leaving the trimming at the top and bottom of each length until last.

1 Hang the drop on the wall, butting it up to the last full drop hung. Then drape the paper over the frame and brush it gently into the top of the architrave (trim).

2 Take the paperhanger's scissors and make a diagonal release cut through the paper into the external corner of the frame. Be careful not to tear the damp paper.

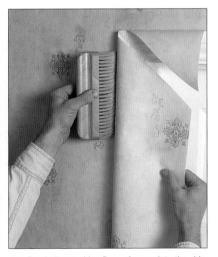

3 Brush the resulting flaps of paper into the side and top of the architrave, using a dabbing action with the bristles of the paperhanger's brush. Crease them with the scissors.

4 Trim the paper flush with the architrave using a sharp craft knife, or pull it back gently and cut it with the scissors. Hang the next drop around the other side of the frame.

AROUND WINDOWS

Hanging wallpaper around a window that is set flush in the wall with a decorative frame around it requires a similar technique to that used for papering around a door. However, many windows are set into the wall to leave a shallow recess that must be tackled in a slightly different manner. Fortunately, any small mishaps or irregularities in the papering around a window can often be concealed by curtains or blinds.

Hang the first length overlapping the window, matching the pattern to the last length hung. Smooth the paper on to the wall, then make horizontal cuts into the corners of the reveal – the first level with the top of the window sill, and the second level with the top of the reveal.

Locate the corners of the window sill and make diagonal release cuts toward these points so that the paper can be eased around the shape of the sill. Brush the paper below the sill on to the wall, and trim to fit. Brush the remaining flap of paper around the corner into the reveal and trim to fit against the window frame. Make sure air bubbles are expelled, but do not apply too much pressure. If the overlap is not deep enough for the reveal, hang a narrow strip to fit between its edge and the window frame.

Cut an oversized patch to fit the head of the reveal, matching the pattern to the paper above the reveal. Make a release cut in the outer corner, then slip the pasted patch into place. Tuck

1 Drape the paper over the window reveal, and make horizontal cuts at top and bottom so that the paper can be brushed into the reveal. Cut only as far as the corners of the reveal.

the edges of the patch under the paper above and inside the reveal, and trim through both layers with a wavy stroke. Peel back the paper to remove the waste and brush down firmly – the joint should be almost invisible. Complete the rest of the window in the same way, hanging short lengths above and below the reveal. Lengths above the window can be brushed into the reveal complete, provided that it is not deep and the edge is square. With a deep reveal, or one where the edge is not square, cut strips to fit the reveal, turning them slightly on to the face of the wall, then overlap their edges with drops hung on the face. Make a wavy cut through both layers, as before, remove the waste and brush flat.

2 Cut along the top of the window sill and make diagonal release cuts around the sill.

3 Brush the remaining flap of wallpaper into the reveal and trim to fit.

4 Ease back the paper, and cut and fit a patch in the corner of the reveal.

5 Cut through both layers and remove the waste to create an unobtrusive butt join.

6 Hang short lengths above and below the window, matching the pattern.

7 Cut lengths long enough to be brushed into the reveal at the top.

AROUND SWITCHPLATES

Before wallpapering around sockets and switches, turn off the electricity supply and hang the paper over the fitting. Press it firmly against the faceplate so that you can see a clear impression and make a pencil mark 6mm (¼in) in from each corner. Make diagonal cuts to each pencil mark with scissors, trimming the flaps of paper 6mm (¼in) in from the outer edge of the faceplate.

Loosen the screws of the faceplate and ease it from the wall, then use a paperhanger's brush to gently push the flaps of paper behind the faceplate. Push the faceplate back into position and tighten its screws. Wipe off any adhesive from the fitting and allow the paste to dry before restoring the power.

1 Turn off the electricity supply. Use a pencil to mark the corners on the paper where it overhangs the fitting.

2 Make a diagonal cut from the centre to each corner of the faceplate. Loosen the screws and pull the faceplate back.

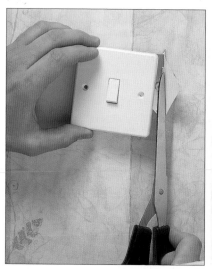

3 Trim the flaps of paper and push them under the edges of the loosened faceplate. Retighten the screws.

AROUND LIGHT FITTINGS

If there is a ceiling rose, turn off the electricity supply before brushing the paper over the casing and then locate its exact centre with your finger. Make a small cut in the paper at this point and gently pull the pendant through the cut, taking care not to tear the paper.

Ease the paper around the shape of the rose by making a series of small radial cuts from the centre of the rose to the edge of the casing. Smooth the paper into place on the ceiling around the rose and finish hanging the rest of the paper. Crease the paper into the edge of the rose before restoring the electricity supply. The paper can be trimmed neatly with a knife once the paste has dried but turn the electricity supply off again before doing this. Where there is a large ceiling centrepiece, it is easier to hang and trim the paper if you plan your starting point so that a join runs through the middle of the fitting. Make radial cuts as for a normal rose to fit the paper up to the edges of the centrepiece.

WALL LIGHT FITTINGS

Turn off the electricity supply and remove the fitting. Bind the wires with electrical insulating or masking tape. Hang the paper to the cable, mark its position on the paper and make a small incision. Feed the cable through the hole, taking care not to tear the paper. Finish hanging the drop and allow the paste to dry before replacing the fitting.

1 Turn off the electricity supply. Make a series of cuts in the paper toward the edge of the ceiling rose. Brush down.

2 Crease the paper around the edge of the rose, then trim neatly with a knife. Finally, brush the paper smooth.

AROUND FIREPLACES

Fireplaces come in a variety of forms; some are very simple and rectangular in outline; others are very ornate. When faced with papering around a simple fireplace, you can use the same techniques as you would for papering around a door frame – make diagonal cuts to the corners and brush the paper into the angles between the fireplace and the wall. However, an ornate frame will require a little more effort.

Hang a full length so that it drapes over the fireplace and match the pattern above the mantel shelf to the last length hung. Lightly brush the paper into the junction of the wall and shelf and trim. Cut inward from the outer corner of the mantel shelf, and support the rest of the length to prevent it from tearing.

Press the paper against the wall at the point where the corner of the shelf meets the wall, gently easing the paper around the contours with your fingers. Make a series of small cuts to allow the paper to lie flat, then use the tips of a paperhanger's brush to mould the paper into the precise shape. Trim each small flap of paper, then crease and trim the paper down the side of the fireplace and wipe any adhesive from the surface.

In some cases, the mantel shelf may span the entire chimney breast (fireplace projection), in which case you need only paper down to the shelf, then cut strips to fit at the sides, making release cuts as necessary to match the shape of the fireplace. You could also use this technique for a fireplace that has a very complex shape to the sides.

1 Hang the drop above the fireplace, draping the paper over the mantel shelf. Brush it into the angle and trim along the back edge.

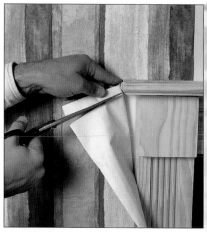

2 Ease the paper around the contours of the mantel shelf by making small release cuts. Brush it into place and trim off the excess.

BEHIND RADIATORS

If a radiator is too heavy to remove, turn it off and allow it to cool completely. Measure and make a note of the position of each wall bracket from the outer edges and top of the radiator, then hang the paper on the wall so that it drapes over the radiator. Match the pattern with the last length hung.

Measure out the position of the wall bracket and make a pencil mark on the wallpaper at this point. Make a vertical slit with scissors from the bottom edge of the paper up to the mark, and use a radiator roller to feed and smooth the paper down on each side of the bracket. Trim the paper neatly along the skirting (baseboard) and wipe off any adhesive left on the face of the wallpaper, skirting and radiator. Repeat for the other bracket.

WALL FITTINGS

When removing wall fittings, mark the position of each screw hole with a wooden match and carefully press the tip through the pasted paper before it is smoothed into place.

1 Use paperhanger's scissors to make a vertical cut from the bottom of the paper in line with the radiator bracket.

2 Carefully feed the paper down behind the radiator with a radiator roller, smoothing it on to the wall at the same time.

HANGING BORDERS

A decorative border can add the finishing touch to a wallpaper or paint scheme. You can choose from a wide variety of patterns, colourways and sizes, all of which are quick and easy to hang. The key to a professional-looking result is to make sure that the border is absolutely straight and hung against accurate guidelines, and that all the joins are neat.

BASIC TECHNIQUES

Use a spirit (carpenter's) level to mark the position of the border on the walls at 300mm (12in) intervals, joining the pencil marks with a long straightedge. Measure from one corner of the wall to the other and add 50mm (2in) for trimming. Paste by brushing out from the centre, and fold concertina-style, leaving the paper to soak for ten minutes. Brush the back of a ready-pasted border with tepid water, rather than immersing it in a trough. A self-adhesive border needs to be re-rolled so that the decorative face is facing outward.

To hang, place 300mm (12in) of the border against the guideline at a time, allowing the folds to drop out as you work. If using a self-adhesive border, peel away the backing paper and smooth it into place. Before cutting and hanging the next length, match the pattern on the roll. Do not attempt to hang a continuous length of border around an external or internal corner; instead use the same technique as for hanging conventional paper.

DEALING WITH CORNERS

1 Draw a guideline for the border on the wall using a spirit (carpenter's) level.

TIPS

• Hang a border by working from right to left if you are right-handed, and left to right if left-handed.
• Positioning a border is easier if the guideline is above a horizontal border, and on the inner edge around windows and doors.
• Hang a border below an uneven ceiling and paint the gap to match.

If you have to use more than one length on a wall, a butt join can be used for borders with a simple repeat pattern. For more complex designs, overlap the two lengths so that the pattern matches exactly and carefully cut around a motif through both layers. When the waste paper has been removed and the cut edges smoothed into place, the join should be almost invisible. Use a seam roller to press down the edges.

2 Fold a pasted border concertina-style so that it is ready to hang and easy to handle.

3 Match the pattern in a corner using a dry length, before cutting and pasting.

CREATING A BUTT JOIN

1 Form a butt join between two lengths of a border that has a simple pattern.

2 Use a seam roller to press edges and joins down firmly.

CREATING AN INVISIBLE JOIN

An intricate pattern gives you the option of disguising a join between lengths of border. Simply overlap the end of one length over the other, matching the patterns accurately, then cut through both layers, following the outline of part of the pattern. Remove the waste and brush down; the join will disappear.

DIVIDING A WALL WITH A BORDER

A border will allow two different wallpaper patterns to be applied to a wall, one above and one below, by concealing the joint between them. Mark a guideline on the wall, approximately 900mm (3ft) from the floor, and hang a length of each design at the same time so that it overlaps the pencil line by 50mm (2in). Before hanging the next lengths, hold a long straightedge on the guideline and cut through both layers of paper with a knife. Remove the waste strips and smooth down the cut edges to form a neat butt joint.

When the room has been papered, the border can then be hung. Centre it over the butt join using an overlap adhesive for vinyl wallcoverings.

AROUND A WINDOW OR DOOR

Draw a horizontal guideline to the full width of the border above the frame, and then mark a vertical guideline down each side. Cut the horizontal length 50mm (2in) longer than required and hang it, making sure that it overlaps the side guidelines evenly.

Add the vertical lengths, overlapping the horizontal strip squarely at the corners. Use the trimming allowance on the vertical lengths to adjust the border so that you will be cutting through the busiest part of the design. Holding a steel rule at a 45-degree angle, cut through both layers of paper from the external to internal corner of the border, using a craft knife. Peel back the cut edges and remove the

waste paper from the wall. Brush the border back into place to create a neat mitred join at each corner.

You can use this technique of making mitred right-angled joins between lengths to allow for changes in floor or ceiling level, or to use the border to

DIVIDING A WALL

1 Hang a drop of each patterned paper so that they overlap the pencil guideline. Work on one pair of drops at a time.

MITRING A CORNER BORDER

1 Mark out horizontal and vertical guidelines for the lengths of border, using a spirit (carpenter's) level.

outline other features such as fireplaces or perhaps even pictures.

In some cases, you might want the border to run along the wall above the stairs. In this situation, the technique of making an angled cut through both layers of the border where they overlap is the same, but the actual angle will be shallower. You need to mark the wall with a pencil guideline that runs parallel to the flight of stairs, then hang the border. Where it overlaps at the top and bottom of the stairs, cut from corner to corner as before and brush flat.

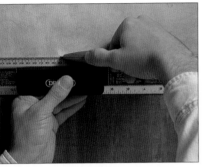

2 Brush the ends of the paper flat, trim through both layers along the guideline and remove the waste. Brush the ends back.

3 When you have completed the wall, centre the border over the butt join between the two papers and wipe away any traces of adhesive.

2 Overlap the ends of the lengths of border and cut through both layers from corner to corner, using a straightedge and sharp knife.

3 Remove the waste pieces of paper and smooth down the cut edges to form a neat mitred join.

PAPERING CEILINGS

Wallpapering a ceiling is not as difficult as it may appear. The techniques used are the same as for walls and there are few obstacles or awkward angles to deal with. Although the job will be easier with two people, it is possible to achieve good results on your own. Adequate access equipment, however, is essential and will make the job very much easier.

ACCESS EQUIPMENT

Before tackling this job, it is important to consider how you plan to reach the ceiling safely. Access equipment will be needed that allows you to hang a full length across the room. Scaffold boards supported at either end by sturdy stepladders or trestles will create a flat, level walkway spanning the full width of the room, and can be adjusted to a working height to suit you. Use two boards tied together for a distance of more than 1.5m (5ft) and provide support in the centre.

PAPERING SEQUENCES

Plan the papering sequence so that a paper that has a definite pattern is centralized across the room. A sloping ceiling can be papered either to match the ceiling or the walls, but do not attempt to hang a single length down the sloping surface on to the wall below. Treat the wide angle between the two surfaces as an internal corner.

HANGING THE FIRST LENGTH

Assemble your work platform across the main window of the room. Ceilings should be papered by hanging lengths across the room parallel to the window, working away from the light so that you are not in your own shadow and daylight will not emphasize the joins between lengths.

To mark a guideline for the first length, measure one roll width less 25mm (1in) out from each corner and drive in a nail at each point. Tie a taut, chalked length of string between the nails, then snap the string against the ceiling to create a guide for the first length. If hanging paper on a white ceiling, make sure you use coloured chalk to coat the string. ►

HANDLING PAPER

As long lengths of paper are often needed for a ceiling, fold these concertina-style after pasting. When papering, they are easier to handle if you support them with a spare roll of wallpaper.

1 Measure out from each corner to a distance equal to the width of a roll and mark the positions with nails.

2 Tie a chalked length of string between the nails, making sure it is taut. Snap it against the ceiling to leave a chalk guideline.

3 Hang the first length against the chalk line, brushing it into place as you go. If possible, have someone else support the folded paper.

4 Use the bristles of a paperhanger's brush to ease the paper into the angle between the wall and ceiling.

5 Use the back of the scissors blade to crease the paper. Then pull it back from the ceiling and trim along the long edge. Brush the cut edge back into place firmly. Treat each end of the length in the same manner.

Cut the first strip of paper to length, allowing an extra 100mm (4in) for trimming, then paste and fold it concertina-style. Place one end so that about half of the trimming allowance laps on to the wall and the edge of the paper is aligned with the chalk line, then brush it firmly into place.

If you are papering around a bay window or alcove, make diagonal release cuts at the external corners to allow the paper to lay flat. Brush the paper into the side wall of the recess and trim the edges to fit along the edge of the ceiling.

Once the first length of wallpaper is in position, crease and trim the long edge into the angle between the wall and ceiling first, followed by each end, using normal wallpapering techniques. Continue hanging lengths of paper across the ceiling, trimming their ends where they meet the walls. Finally, cut the last length roughly to the width required, making sure you allow 25mm (1in) for trimming along the edge of the paper. Hang and trim it in the same manner as the first length.

DEALING WITH PROBLEM AREAS

If you are faced with papering around a bay window or an alcove, make diagonal release cuts in the paper at the external corners of the recess to allow the paper to lay flat against the ceiling. Brush the paper into the side walls of the recess, crease it and trim it to fit along the edges of the ceiling.

PAPERING AN ALCOVE

ABOVE: Paper into a bay window or an external corner by making a diagonal cut to ease the paper around the external angle.

A SLOPING CEILING

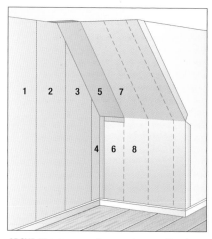

ABOVE: The sequence for papering a wall and a sloping ceiling. Do not try to hang a complete length on the sloping surface and down the wall.

PAPERING ARCHES

If possible, arrange your starting position on the wall containing the arch so that you will be left with an even width to fill between the arch and each full-width drop on each side of it.

1 Trim away excess paper from the arch to leave a trimming allowance of 25mm (1in).

This will ensure a balanced appearance. Hang the paper so that it overlaps the arch, matching the pattern to the last length hung, then trim off the waste to within 25mm (1in) from the edge of the arch. Brush the trimming allowance on to the inner face of the arch, making right-angled cuts into the paper every 12mm (½in) around the curve of the arch so that it lays flat. Paper across the rest of the arch, length by length, using the same method of cutting to cope with the curved edge.

For the inner face, cut a strip of paper 35mm (1¼in) wider than the arch. If the paper has a definite pattern, use two strips with a butt joint at the highest point. Align the manufactured edge of the cut strip with one edge of the arch and trim the other edge with a knife once the paper has been smoothed into place.

2 Make right-angled cuts to ease the paper around the curve of the arch.

3 Paper the inner face of the arch last, joining strips at the highest point.

PAPERING STAIRWELLS

When working in stairwells, safety is the main priority. Access equipment suitable for use on stairs may be hired, but you can also construct your own safe work platform.

ORDER OF WORK

Hang the longest length first, and work upward from the foot of the stairs.

Hang the top half of each length, but leave the rest of the folded length hanging while you move the work platform out of the way. Then smooth the lower half of each length into place.

When measuring lengths for a well wall, make sure that you allow for the gradient of the stairs.

Tackle the head wall next, hanging the top portions of the two or three drops needed, leaving the remainder of the folded lengths hanging. Adjust the work platform so that the planks rest on a stair or ladder and are supported by a ladder at the bottom. Smooth the lower portions of the lengths on to the head wall, and trim neatly in line with the hallway ceiling. Hang lengths along the lower head wall from the foot of the stairs.

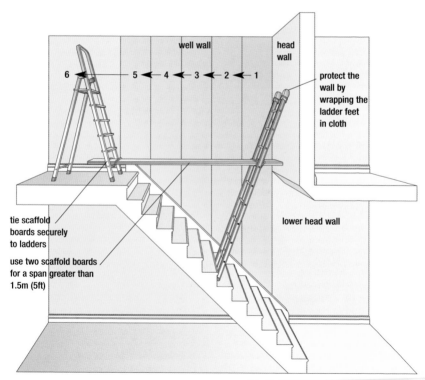

ABOVE: How to construct a platform for a straight staircase and order of papering for the well wall.

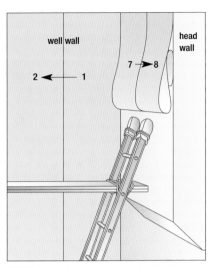

ABOVE: The order of papering for the head wall of a stairwell. Note that the ends of the straight ladder have been padded to prevent damage to the wall. Adjust the access equipment before brushing the lower half of the wall.

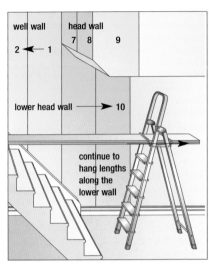

ABOVE: The order of papering for the lower head wall of a staircase. Work off the foot of the stairs, using a scaffold board and stepladders as necessary. Trim the paper neatly at the angles between ceiling, stairs and wall.

ABOVE: Be especially careful to take accurate measurements. Mistakes can be costly when working with very long lengths.

ABOVE: Hang the longest length first and work upward from the foot of the stairs. Hang the top half of each length first.

COMMON PROBLEMS

Inadequate preparation and poor papering techniques, rather than faults with the paper itself, are the cause of most wallpapering problems. Some minor mistakes such as air bubbles are quite easy to remedy, but if the problem is extensive, it is better to strip off the affected area and start again.

DEALING WITH BUBBLES

Bubbles that remain after the paste has dried are caused by not allowing the paper to soak for long enough, not having brushed out the

paper properly, or by poor preparation, which prevents the paper from sticking to the wall.

With a small bubble, you may be able to cut a slit in the paper and inject a little paste behind it with a syringe. Then press the paper down and carefully wipe off any excess paste.

For a larger bubble, make two diagonal cuts with a sharp knife. Carefully peel back the flaps and use a small paintbrush to apply paste to the back of each. Press the flaps back against the wall and brush flat, again wiping off any excess paste.

REPAIRING A BUBBLE

1 When faced with the occasional large bubble in a papered surface, make diagonal cuts across its face with a sharp knife. Then peel back the resulting flaps.

2 Apply more paste to the wall or the backs of the cut flaps of paper. Press back into place and brush down firmly. If there are lots of bubbles, it may be better to replace the drop.

REPAIRING TEARS

Often, tears are not as bad as they look. If the tear is small, carefully apply some overlap adhesive to the torn piece and ease it back into place with the tips of a brush.

When faced with a large tear in wallpaper, remove loose and damaged paper by tearing it gently from the wall. Tear, rather than cut, a patch from a new piece of paper so that the pattern matches the surrounding area, then feather the edge by tearing away a 6mm (¼in) strip from the back. Paste the patch and lightly brush it into place.

With a vinyl wallcovering, cut a patch so that the pattern matches the surrounding area and tape it to the wall over the damage. Cut through both layers to form a square, remove the damaged vinyl from the wall, then paste and fit the patch.

REPAIRING DAMAGED WALLCOVERINGS

1 Carefully tear away any loose or damaged wallpaper, feathering the edges.

2 Make a matching patch by carefully tearing the paper. Feather the edges and stick it down.

REPAIRING VINYL

1 Cut out damaged vinyl and a new patch taped on to the wall to match in one go.

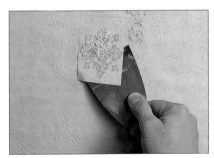

2 Remove the old vinyl from within the cut square and apply the patch.

OTHER WALLPAPERING TIPS

By and large, hanging a wallcovering is a straightforward process which, in most cases, will go without a hitch. However, now and again you may come across a difficult situation that needs overcoming. Some of the most common problems are covered here, and if you follow the techniques you will be able to give your decorative scheme a professional-looking finish.

LONG LENGTHS

In the stairwell the drop from ceiling to floor will be considerable in places. Get someone to support the weight of the wallcovering while you hang the top portion.

BULKY OVERLAPS

Overlapped edges can create bulky seams in relief and embossed wallpapers. Feather the trimming allowance by carefully tearing down the edge, then flatten the torn paper with a seam roller before hanging the overlapping length.

GAPS IN SEAMS

Paper shrinking as it dries, due to poor pasting technique or poor butt joins, can cause gaps at the seams. To avoid this, disguise the gaps with a fine felt-tipped pen, paint or crayon in a similar shade to the base colour.

CURLING EDGES

These are caused by inadequate pasting, paste drying out during hanging or, on overlapped vinyl, the wrong paste having been used. Lift the edge of the paper with the back of a knife blade and apply a small amount of paste with a fine brush. Smooth the paper firmly into place with a damp sponge. For overlapping edges on vinyl wallpaper, use vinyl overlap adhesive.

POOR PATTERN MATCH

Usually the result of inaccurate cutting and hanging, patterns not matching may also be caused by variations in the paper along the seams. Check the whole batch and return faulty rolls to the retailer. Straight-match patterns can be difficult to match, especially in internal corners where the edge has been trimmed. Use a level to check that prominent motifs are level across the corner.

SHINY PATCHES

Brushing matt finish wallpapers too vigorously can cause shiny patches. Normally, they cannot be removed, but rubbing gently with a piece of fresh white bread may disguise them. Bread is also useful for removing greasy fingermarks from non-washable papers.

STAINS ALONG SEAMS

Paste that has been allowed to dry on the face of the paper can result in stains. These are difficult to remove, but if the paper is washable, try wiping with a sponge and a solution of mild detergent. Bear this in mind while working and sponge off splashes before they have a chance to dry.

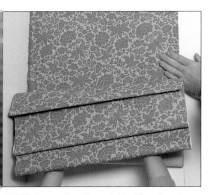

ABOVE: Supporting the weight of long lengths will help prevent the wallpaper tearing.

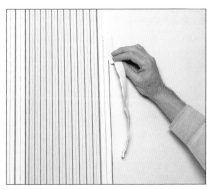

ABOVE: Feather the edge of relief wallpaper at external and internal corners.

ABOVE: Disguise gaps with a felt-tipped pen, a crayon or watercolour paint.

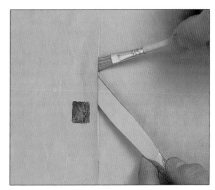

ABOVE: Apply wallpaper adhesive to curling edges with a fine brush.

ABOVE: Use a spirit (carpenter's) level to check that motifs are level across a corner.

ABOVE: Rubbing with a ball of white bread may make shiny patches less obvious.

INDEX